The Basics of Food Safety

This book is designed to help you learn the basics of food safety so you will be able to pass the Level 2 examination with ease.

It is also intended as a reference book to keep handy in all kitchens so everyone, in a food business, large or small, understands the importance of complying with the law.

by

Susie Ellis

Contents:

Chapter 1: Introduction

Let's see what you already know…

Preparing food for the public is a totally different ball game to cooking for friends and family. Even if you are not charging money the law applies & the penalties are severe if someone becomes ill or there is the potential for illness in your facilities.

What is unsafe, or a hazard to food safety, in this picture?

Answers:

Dog spittle plus sharing food with animals contaminates your hands

Dirty washing up & flies

Chicken cooling on window sill – flies etc getting in open window

Kitchen cleaner beside food – chemical contaminant

Raw meat above cooked meat – drip down contamination causing food poisoning

Mop & cleaning bucket in kitchen – needs a separate area

Dirty bin

Fridge door open

Plate of hot food near dirty washing up

It's not rocket science – you already know all this

There may be 12 chapters but it is really all the same stuff looked at from 12 different angles

Benefits & costs

Everyone who works with food has a responsibility to make sure that food does not cause harm to consumers.

As a food handler there are things that you can do to ensure that the food you make, serve or sell, is safe to eat.

The maintenance of good standards of food hygiene can benefit a food business & poor standards result in significant costs.

What are the benefits? As a business/customer/candidate/employee/
- Good reputation
- Satisfied customers
- Loyal customers
- Legal compliance
- Less food waste & controlled running costs
- Reduced risk of food poisoning
- Pleasant place to work
- Motivated workforce
- Job security

What would be the costs?
- Bad reputation
- Dissatisfied customers – more complaints
- Loss of profits
- More food waste & higher running costs
- Outbreaks of food poisoning
- Legal action & penalties
- Unpleasant & potentially unhealthy place to work
- Demotivated workforce
- Redundancy due to closure of the business

Important terms:

Food safety
Food poisoning/food borne illness
Contamination
Hazard analysis
HACCP

Don't worry if you don't know the exact definitions all will be clear by the end of this book.

Food safety:

What is the definition of food safety?

The protection of consumer health and well-being by safeguarding food from anything that can cause harm

Food poisoning & food borne illness:

Types of illness caused by eating contaminated food

Food poisoning is caused by eating food contaminated by:
- Harmful bacteria
- Harmful substances – e.g. poisonous plants or fungi, chemical, metals etc.

What are the symptoms of food poisoning?
- Stomach cramps
- Nausea
- Diarrhoea
- Vomiting
- Dehydration
- Fever
- Abdominal pain
- Headache

Food poisoning & food borne illness 'at risk' groups:

Generally, the symptoms of food poisoning are unpleasant & usually last from 24 hours to several days occasionally longer.

For most of us the effects are not serious but for some people it can be life-threatening.

What groups of people are particularly at risk from food poisoning or food borne illness?

- Very young people
- Elderly people
- Pregnant women & unborn babies
- People who are ill or recovering from illness

They are at greater risk because their immune systems are not working well & they cannot fight off illness

Contamination:

The presence in food of any harmful or objectionable substance or object

Hazard:

Anything that could cause harm to consumers

HACCAP:

HACCAP [Hazard Analysis Critical Control Point] is a formal system that helps food businesses to protect food safety

It is a legal requirement for the majority of food businesses to have a documented food
safety management system based on the principles of HACCP

The documentation & record keeping should be in keeping with the size & nature of the
food business.

Consider how a management system would differ between a large hospital & a small café

In the hospital there will be vulnerable people- sick, young & elderly & is likely to have large numbers of customers & staff

The café will mainly cater for healthy people & maybe have fewer than 10 employees

Therefore documentation & record keeping will be more comprehensive for the hospital kitchen than the café – there is more potential to cause harm if things go wrong.

Chapter 1: Raw meat

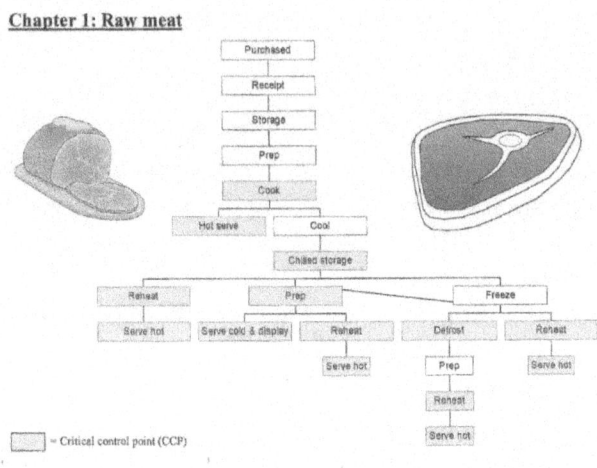

This is an example from part of a HACCAP document & it would cover the company from everything from goods I when they arrive to the cooking of the final product or the sale of it

This is about raw meat & the yellow tags are the critical control points. A business needs to write down the purchase, receipt, storage & prep & then consider how the meat is to be cooked. How hot is the cooking temperature to be, who is going to be cooking it etc?

Then its going to be cooled down & put in storage – there are loads of regulations about cooling which we will go into later in greater detail

The meat is then going to be reheated & served hot or prepped, served cold, displayed, reheated & served hot or chilled frozen defrosted & so on

There are lots of little places where things could go seriously wrong if you don't maintain all the rules applicable to your particular company or setup

STEPS	HAZARDS	CONTROLS	MONITOR
Purchase and Delivery	Harmful bacteria, contamination, poor quality packaging poor temp control	Visual checks, smell feel, packaging, vehicle. Probe check for 5c, use a reputable supplier.	Check invoices, record temp of 5c. Visit suppliers and check vehicles for hygiene and temp control
Storage	Cross contamination, deteriorating quality, beyond dates.	Store in separate covered containers in a designated area or/or fridge at 5c. Correct stock rotation, label and date produce.	Label fridges and designated areas. Record temp of 5c. Label/date products, visually check fridges and areas.
Preparation	Bacterial growth, cross contamination of high risk foods. Contamination of hands surfaces and equipment.	Separate foods during handling and preparation to prevent cross contamination. Good personal hygiene. Sanitise and clean afterwards. Use correct coded boards and work in designated areas.	Visual checks of equipment, work areas and personal hygiene. Up to date training and procedures in place. label work areas.
Cooking Hot serve.	Survival of bacteria. Growth and survival of bacteria.	Cook to >75c for 2 minutes. Keep food at >70c for maximum 2 hours at service.	Probe check and record for >75c Probe check and record for >70c
Cooling.	Growth of bacteria	Cool quickly in designated (shallow bain-marie trays) containers with lids to 10c within 1.5 hours in chiller	Probe check and record for 10c Display loading and operational instructions on chiller

This is what the second or detail page would look like...

Each bullet point from the first image is detailed in writing

For purchase & delivery we identify the hazards as being harmful bacteria, contamination, poor quality packaging, poor temperature control

The controls identified, or what someone has to look out for are: visual checks, smell, feel packaging vehicle. Food must be probe checked for 5°C & reputable supplier must be used

Ongoing monitoring: – check invoices, record temps & make sure the meat did actually arrive at less than 5°C, visit suppliers, check vehicles for hygiene & temp control

In a large business every single step is documented in a similar way to these examples.

In a micro or small business, the law will require you to be able to say this to an Environmental Health Officer. You may not necessarily have to have it written down but you will have to demonstrate that you understand the where the critical controls points occur

Chapter 2: The Law

Now we are going to learn about all the same stuff but from the legal point of view

The role of enforcement officers

Provide food safety advice
*   Inspect food premises
*   Enforce legislation covering food

Powers of enforcement officers

Enter and inspect food and premises
*   Investigate outbreaks of food-borne disease and possible offences
*   Remove suspect food and have it destroyed if it is considered to be unsafe to eat
*   Serve improvement and prohibition notices
*   Take food businesses & food handlers to court for breaking food safety laws

Notices:

A **Hygiene Improvement Notice** is used to require food businesses to improve something substandard – e.g. a broken tap or inadequate record keeping

A **Hygiene Emergency Prohibition Notice** can apply to:-
*   Premises e.g. Prohibiting the use of the premises due to pest infestation
*   Part of the premises e.g. Prohibiting the use of a food store with a broken roof.
*   Equipment e.g. Prohibiting the use of a griddle for cooking burgers that is not working properly.

A **Prohibition Notice** can apply to:

A person e.g. Prohibiting someone who has run a food business unsafely in the past from running one in the future.

Penalties for Non-Compliance

The penalties for non-compliance include:
- Prohibition from using part of a business [equipment, system or area]
- Prohibition from running a food business
- Fines, legal costs & compensation
- Criminal record
- Prison

Here are some examples of issue that an Environmental Health Officer might tackle:

What do you think the answers could be?

A food safety enforcement officer noted the following problems on inspections of food premises.

Problem found	What happened next?
Sandwich shop repeatedly found to have dirty food preparation surfaces. A written notice has previously been served requiring a proper cleaning procedure, which has not been introduced.	
Restaurant – High risk foods on sweet trolley found to be out of temperature control for over four hours.	
Sweet factory which produces mechanically wrapped sweets – staff found smoking and not washing hands afterwards.	
Supermarket – providing staff wash hand basins with domestic bar soap and traditional fabric hand-towels.	
Delicatessen – storing foods such as fruit and tinned foods in a chiller cabinet.	
Meat pie factory found to have heavy rat infestation, with droppings in food storage and production areas	

Choose from the list below the likely action you think the enforcement officer would have taken in each situation. You may choose more than one option for a single problem.

Actions:
Make a comment
Give advice
Send a letter
Serve an Improvement Notice
Prosecute
Close down immediately

What did you choose as your answer?

Answers:

The sandwich shop would be prosecuted as they have had written notices, received reminders but done nothing

The restaurant would be served an improvement notice as high-risk food must not be out in the danger zone for over 4 hours [detailed definitions of 'high risk food' & 'danger zone' will be explained in a later chapter]

The sweet factory would probably receive a letter. Sweets are very high in sugar so they don't harbour bacteria growth easily & they are also wrapped so people's hands don't touch them. You must wash your hands after smoking

The supermarket would probably just be given advice. Liquid soap is preferable to bar soap as bar soap has the potential to harbor bacteria & transfer bacteria from person to person. Paper towels are preferable to fabric ones for the same reason

The delicatessen will receive a comment as it is unnecessary to store tinned food in a chiller cabinet

The meat pie factory would be prosecuted & may well be closed down immediately!

This is a newspaper cutting from several years ago…Tesco was fined £25,000 after one of its flagship stores was found to be infested with mice & selling mouldy food

FINED FOR MOULD ON THE FOOD

By Jonathan Prynn and Isabel Oakeshott

£25,000 blow for store giant

TESCO has been fined £25,000 after one of its flagship stores was found to be infested with mice and selling mouldy food.

The fine, one of the biggest ever handed out for breaches of food safety rules, will come as a huge embarrassment to Britain's biggest supermarket chain.

The store at New Malden in south-west London, one of Tesco's biggest, was taken to court by council inspectors following a series of customer complaints. Details emerged today of an extraordinary litany of failures at the 10-year-old superstore. The company was fined:

● £5,000 for selling a mouldy apple turnover seven days past its sell-by date.
● £2,000 for selling Gouda cheese past its sell-by date.
● £4,000 for selling mouldy Thai rice.
● £2,000 each for failing to store Clipper coffee and cereals "in a hygienic manner". Rodents had nibbled packaging.
● £5,000 for failing to keep rodents out of food storage areas. Merton council officials found "rodent faeces and food… gnawed by rodents and the existence of food and water sources within easy reach of rodents". The failings had not been put right a month later despite warnings.
● £5,000 for not keeping fridge cabinets at the right temperature and for not logging customer complaints adequately.

The fine for breaches of the Food Safety Act, food safety regulations and

Continued on Page 2

Cadburys was responsible for a salmonella outbreak

Dairy Milk bars on the production line at the Cadbury's factory RICHARD LEA-HAIR

Cadbury to consider payouts for victims of salmonella outbreak

By Martin Hickman
Consumer Affairs
Correspondent

Cadbury has said it will consider compensating victims of salmonella poisoning after health officials named its chocolate as the prime suspect for an outbreak earlier this year.

Britain's biggest confectioner promised to "take seriously" any case arising from a mysterious spate of infections throughout the spring, which put two children in hospital.

The Health Protection Agency (HPA) concluded that consumption of infected Cadbury's products was the "most credible explanation" for 37 cases of salmonella poisoning reported between March and July this year.

The statement is another blow to the reputation of Cadbury – against whom the Food Standards Agency and local authorities are considering a prosecution for breach of health and safety legislation.

The company took five months to inform the Food Standards Agency that salmonella had infected chocolate crumb at its Marlbrook plant in Herefordshire in January.

Even then, as it withdrew one million bars of seven products from sale last month, the FTSE 100 company was insisting its chocolate was safe to eat.

Yesterday, the HPA said that of 49 non-travel-related "primary cases" of Salmonella Montevideo since 1 March, 37 were of the same strain of salmonella, SmvdX07, that was found in Cadbury's products including Dairy Milk.

Detailed food histories for 15 of the patients – whose average age was two – discounted many common sources of food poisoning such as eating out and takeaways. The only strong link was that 13 of them had eaten Cadbury products.

During their inquiry, health officials considered the distribution of cases across the country and the onset of the illness while the infected chocolate was on sale. The HPA announced: "The outbreak control team concluded that consumption of products made by Cadbury Schweppes was the most credible explanation for the outbreak."

Cadbury – which microbiologists criticised for selling the bars after tests first discovered salmonella in January – refused to say whether it agreed with the HPA's conclusion.

But it said in a statement: "Clearly we regret that people have been unwell. We have already announced that we have changed our protocol [scrapping the company's previous policy that chocolate with low levels of salmonella was safe to sell] because for us the consumer's desire for no risk at all is paramount and any product showing any traces of salmonella will be destroyed."

A spokeswoman added: "If any people come forward we will take their situation seriously and consider their case."

The HPA estimates that it is told of between one-fifth and one-third of all salmonella cases, suggesting the total number of cases linked to Cadbury was between 111 and 185.

Dewhurst were fined £1000 for selling a mouldy pork pie & displaying for sale a mouldy cheese. Dewhurst were also fined £33,400 for hygiene offences at its Leamington Spa & Warwick shops… & the other two cuttings are equally as shocking

You can see the seriousness of not complying with the Law!

Due diligence defence fails Dewhurst

Dewhurst have been fined £1,000 after being found guilty of selling a mouldy pork pie and displaying for sale a mouldy cheese, contrary to section 8 of the Food Act 1984.

The company pleaded not guilty to the charges, brought by Doncaster MBC, and in defence attempted to plead due diligence claiming that the commission of the offences was due to the act or default of another person, namely the shop manager, under the provisions of section 100 of the Food Act 1984.

The details of the defence were read to the magistrates, citing Tesco Supermarkets Ltd vs Nattrass and Beckett vs Kingston Bros (Butchers) Ltd. The company's area manager for the shop in question attempted to prove the presence of an effective management control system for stock control and shop procedures.

The company had cited the procedures laid down in the company instructions and shop cash record book, its 'Red Book', which contains details of the operations its staff should carry out, including food hygiene. It claimed this constituted a proper system of management control.

The magistrates found that simply asking an employee to read a procedure and signing to say they have read it was insufficient supervision and training. In addition the stock management procedures laid down in the 'Red Book' were shown to be inadequate. No details were given on date coding of cheese for stock rotation purposes, nor for wrapping and re-wrapping of cheese which had been displayed for sale.

The shop manager had only been working in the shop for a week as relief manager, although he was a full-time manager at another branch in the area. He was therefore not fully conversant with the operating procedures in the shop.

Dewhurst was fined £500 on each of the two charges and the council was awarded £566 costs. The manager of the shop was conditionally discharged for a year after pleading guilty to both charges.

Dewhurst fine: Dewhurst butchers has been fined a total of £33,400 for hygiene offences at its Leamington Spa and Warwick shops.

Costs of £1,646 were awarded to Warwick DC, which presented 23 charges.

EHOs found insanitary premises and contraventions including soiled cleaning cloths, poorly maintained chopping blocks, soiled food containers, meat stored on dirty floors, a filthy toilet, no proper facilities for hand washing, lack of fly screening and unsatisfactory arrangements for storing outdoor clothing. Warwick says the use of sawdust featured significantly in defaults under regulation 25.

Four months for hot-dog man

A hot-dog salesman in Liverpool who defied an Emergency Prohibition Order was given a four-months jail sentence — suspended for two years.

Principal EHO Tom Liddell served the notice under the Food Safety Act 1990 after an inspection uncovered filthy conditions and a car being repaired on the premises. The business involved a fleet of mobile trolleys selling hot dogs which were prepared on these premises.

The notice was duly served and posted up on 40 Henry Street on 27 April. However, Mr Liddell was tipped off that the hot dog business proprietor, Brian Hardman, was still producing food from the premises.

A visit from Mr Liddell and Assistant CEHO John O'Neill confirmed that this was the case. The officers took photographs, which were presented in court, and made sure that all food was thrown away. They also arranged for a special collection of the bins by the Cleansing Depot.

The sentence was welcomed by Liverpool's EHOs. The premises were filthy, with water ponding on the floor, trade waste and refuse in piles, a broken window, and open food throughout.

Said John O'Neill after the case: 'This highlights the need for continued vigilance by enforcement officers, even when the Court has issued an Emergency Prohibition Order, particularly in the case of premises which only open in the evening or at weekends.'

Ban imposed on food-shop owner

Magistrates are seeking to use to their powers under the Food Safety Act 1990. The manager of a kebab-manufacturing business in Southend, Essex, has had a Prohibition Order made against him by Rochford and Southend-on-Sea Magistrates Court, preventing him from participating in the management of any food business.

This is the first such order to be made in Southend and one of only half a dozen such orders to have been served in the UK, however, as the most recent one was reported in last week's issue (EHN, 14 February, page 7). The signs are that they will be rather more widely used from now on.

Southend-on-Sea Principal EHO Alan Herbert told EHN that routine investigation of the premises — the Moon and Star on the Temple Farm Industrial Estate — found a mouse infestation along with serious food hygiene contraventions. Sacks of risks were contaminated by mouse droppings, the badly worn floor could not be cleaned effectively, the industrial refrigerator had a filthy floor and dirty wall fixtures, and even the delivery van was insanitary and incapable of being cleaned effectively.

Magistrates ordered the infested risks to be destroyed. When the case came to court, Ibrahim Kersgo was fined a lots of £1,950 for offences under the Food Hygiene (General) Regulations 1970 and the Food Safety Act 1990. Costs of £450 were awarded to the council.

Food Handler – Legal Requirements

This is all about you…

Keep yourself clean
- Keep the workplace clean
- Protect food from contamination or anything that could cause harm
- Follow good personal hygiene practices – e.g. hand washing
- Wear appropriate protective clothing
- Tell your employer if you are suffering from or are a carrier of a food-borne illness

It is your responsibility to tell your employer if you have had sickness &/or diarrhoea if you are working with food & we will cover that in great detail in a later chapter

You won't be allowed to work as a food handler if you are the carrier of a food borne illness. Some large institutions will ask you to complete a form at interview & if they are suspicious about where you last worked or travelled to or from, they may send you off to the Doctor for a stool sample

Record Keeping – HACCAP Requirement

It is a legal requirement that certain records are kept – these are needed to show that the steps in the production & sale of food, that are critical to safety, are being controlled.

Records might include refrigerated storage, cooking & hot holding temperatures, cleaning records, staff training records, pest control, goods in / delivery temperatures.

Record keeping ensures the business complies with the law & provides the evidence of how the food is produced & handled.

It is essential you know what you are doing & why & keep accurate records.

Let your supervisor know if there any problems & make sure there is a record that you have informed your supervisor or line manager. It is your responsibility to report a problem.

Due Diligence

A food business must be able to demonstrate that it has done *everything* within its power to safeguard consumer health

"Due Diligence" can be used as a defence by the food business accused of breaking food safety law.

A business must be able to demonstrate that it has done *everything* within its power to safeguard consumer health.

The majority of food businesses must have a HACCP based food safety management system, but to demonstrate "Due Diligence", a business would need to demonstrate how this works in practice – i.e. Provide evidence of record keeping, monitoring procedures, cleaning schedules etc

For example, let's say a commercial kitchen restaurant becomes infested with mice but the owner of the kitchen has employed the services of a pest control company. The restaurant would have to produce the pest control contract & payment records to the court to prove "Due Diligence" at law. The pest control company would be found responsible & prosecuted ~ they would have to pay the resulting fine or loss of business.

Chapter 3a: Food Safety Hazards

This is all the same stuff once again but looked at from yet another point of view

Three types of Hazards caused by contaminants:

- physical
- chemical
- biological

We are now going to focus on food hazards & how the risk of food poisoning & food borne disease can be contained.

Contaminants are food safety hazards – you need to be able to recognise them & identify whether they are physical, chemical or biological

Some physical contaminants are: piece of packaging, staple, paperclip, mouse dropping*, insect, hair, washer, piece of glass, plaster**, pen top, jewellery, soil, leaf twig

* could be biological too
** read more in Chapter 11

Physical & Chemical contamination

Contamination can occur at any stage from field to fork!

Physical contamination is objectionable because it can be seen by the consumer causing broken teeth, choking, cuts

Chemical contamination may cause severe vomiting in the short term but in the long term it can be responsible for serious illness such as cancer & damage organs e.g. liver, kidneys, brain

Food Poisoning is caused by:

- micro-organisms:
    - bacteria
    - viruses
    - moulds and fungi
- natural poisons in food itself
- chemicals/metals

Before we examine micro-organisms in detail let's think about natural poisons in the food itself.

Natural Poisons:

Wild mushrooms:
We would not eat a wild mushroom before it had been identified as being edible by an expert

Green potatoes:
The humble potato is an example of a food we eat on a daily basis that can contains poisons. Solanine is the chemical that builds up in green skins & sprouting tips. It is very important, therefore, to store potatoes in dark well-ventilated containers to prevent the development of solanine. When preparing potatoes make sure any sprouts or green patches are cut completely out.

Red kidney beans:
Another example of a natural poison is hemagglutinin in red kidney beans. This is the chemical that produces very severe food poisoning symptoms if consumed. These beans are only made safe by soaking them for 12 hours followed by 1.5 hours of boiling

You cannot see bacteria & viruses not can you smell or taste them.

A micro-organism is a very tiny living thing. There are different types of micro-organisms associated with food borne illnesses

Bacteria, which is a single celled micro-organism which is the most common cause of food poisoning

Viruses, which are even smaller than bacteria carried on food & in water

& **Parasites** that live on other organisms

Whereas it might be possible to see some parasites like roundworm, flatworms & flukes that affect foods of animal origin, bacteria & viruses are not visible to the naked eye & you can fit thousands on a pin head.

As a food handler you must learn to control these hazards

Bacteria live in & on our bodies & are everywhere in the natural world

Sources of bacteria known to cause food poisoning include:

- Raw food
- Meat poultry eggs fish
- The outside of fruit & vegetables
- Pests & pets
- Air
- Dirt/soil
- Water
- Dust
- Refuse & waste
- People

Bacteria live in huge quantities in our intestines & come out in faeces. This happens in everyone not just in people who are ill. Bacteria are also found on skin & can come from contaminated clothing

Raw food
Do you think it's safe to eat raw meat? raw eggs? raw fish? raw shellfish?

There are risks associated with eating any food raw but the careful sourcing of ingredients & preparation of food for consumption can help control some of the risks

Raw meat

In rare beef bacteria do not occur within the flesh of the animal unless they are very sick & then they would not be allowed in the human food chain. Most of the bacteria associated with meat comes from the gut & the gut contents & faeces. They get onto meat when it is cut or butchered by contaminated equipment of surfaces. When the meat is cooked adequately all the bacteria on the outside surfaces will be killed & if you use a clean knife to slice the meat it will be safe to eat even when it is rare in the middle.

Burgers however are made from meat with many cut surfaces. Contamination will have travelled all through the meat & it will be necessary to thoroughly cook it all the way through

Another point to consider is that burgers & sausages are made from processed meat. In an abattoir the very last thing that happens when the meat has been jointed, & cut from the bone, is that the carcasses are shot blasted to remove any organs still clinging to the bone. This is when the intestines burst & faeces spread all through the food

Raw eggs

The contamination of eggs with salmonella occurs from two sources; firstly, from chicken faeces on the shell & secondly from the bacteria that inhabit the oviduct within the chicken where the eggs are formed. Bacteria can occur within the white as well as the yolk. It is safer to use 'Lion' brand eggs in the UK as these come from schemes that are tested & ensured salmonella free. Some foreign imports that come without these schemes have been associated with infection in the last few years.

Raw fish & shellfish
Certain shellfish, bivalve molluscs, oysters, mussels & clams can be implicated in food poisoning cases & one of the reasons is the way they eat. They are filter feeders & they filter huge volumes of water. If there are any bacteria or viruses in the water they will accumulate in the filter within the shellfish. Raw fish & shellfish *can* be safe to eat but you need to find sources living in clean water or those subject to depuration ~ particularly those eaten raw such as oysters which are not subject to cooking that would kill any micro organisms

Water
Water comes under food safety regulations as well as foodstuffs. The state of our seas now mean that it is very difficult to get clean shellfish so many are farmed.

Three types of Bacteria:

- pathogenic – cause illness
- helpful – used to make beer, cheese, yoghurt, etc.
- spoilage – cause food to perish or rot

Pathogenic micro-organisms linked to food poisoning:

At this basic level you do not have to know everything about each bacteria in detail, but you must know why bacteria must be controlled.

We're just going to look at the six main culprits

- Campylobacter jejuni
- Staphylococcus aureus
- Bacillus cereus
- Salmonella
- E. coli O157 H7
- Clostridium perfringens
- Norovirus

Campylobacter jejuni is the most common cause of food poisoning in the UK. It is associated with raw meat, commonly found on raw poultry. It causes severe food poisoning lasting from 1 – 10 days & the onset time is 1 – 5 days

Staphylococcus aureus comes from people. A good way of remembering it is the word staph / staff [employees] & mainly from the skin of carriers which is 1/3 of the population.
It is also found on cut or damaged skin & lesions, nose, hair, ears & mouth.

This is why you need to keep cuts covered with a waterproof dressing or plaster – these have to coloured blue in a food environment to aid detection if they fall off. It causes food poisoning by producing a toxin within the food as the bacteria multiply. Toxins are poisons produced by bacteria. When the toxin is in the stomach it is vomited back out within a couple of hours of eating the contaminated food. The control is to ensure the bacteria cannot multiply prior to eating. Keeping food refrigerated will restrict both bacteria multiplication & toxin production. Multiplication of bacteria will be explained in the next chapter but note that toxins are not destroyed by cooking.

Bacillus cereus is often associated with rice & cereals. It has a very special way of surviving unfavourable environments by the formation of a spore. Spore formation will be explained in the next chapter. One type of food poisoning causes illness in a similar way to Staphylococcus aureus, namely a formation of a toxin within the food. The symptoms are mainly vomiting & abdominal cramps with a quick onset. The second type is caused by the formation of a toxin in the intestines & is therefore more associated with diarrhoea & has a longer onset time before the symptoms become apparent

Salmonella can be found in human & animal guts, pests & sewage. The toxin leaking out of the cell has a corrosive like effect on the intestines & the body responds by expelling the infection ~ hence diarrhoea. Some of the cells do not break open but are excreted in a livable viable form. This is what happens during the illness but can continue once the symptoms have all gone; so that person can then become a carrier. Salmonella food poisoning can be transmitted via the faecal/oral route; by affected people not washing their hands properly after going to the lavatory & then touching uncontaminated food. In food poisoning cases such a salmonella typhi food handlers may be required to give faecal samples as part of the process of trying to identify the source of an outbreak. You will remember from the law chapter, that as a food handler, you must tell your supervisor if you have food poisoning, or the symptoms of food poisoning, even if it was when you were away from work & you think you have now recovered.

E. coli O157 H7 is a very nasty bacteria that can be fatal by causing kidney failure, particularly in children, the elderly & unwell people. It originates in the gut of animals, particularly cattle, & is associated with undercooked meat. An outbreak in Scotland at the end of 1996 caused around 500 cases & killed 18 people. A butcher, prized for his products, was well respected within his community but allowed raw meat to contaminate cooked products which were consumed & caused the illness. The butchers name was John Farr & not only was the contamination a problem but when it came to court it was discovered that the cleaning products he used were not adequate. When asked he said "we always use the green liquid" – this turned out to be a detergent & not a disinfectant. We will cover cleaning in chapter 9

Clostridium perfringens ~ the origin is in the gut, dirt & soil. It causes diarrhoea & abdominal pain 12 – 24 hours after ingesting. It tends to flourish where there is restricted or no oxygen so it is often associated with stews, rolled joints & other dense products. Clostridium perfringens is a spore forming bacteria [as is bacillus cereus] see next chapter

Norovirus originates in gut, sewage & contaminated water. It causes vomiting diarrhoea & abdominal pains, sometimes headache caused by dehydration & fever, 24-48 hours after ingestion. It is one of the most common causes of infectious gastro enteritis. Transmitted by faecal/oral route & commonly involves food eaten raw such a shellfish, vegetables, salad & fruit or by drinking unclean water. Norovirus does not rely on food to survive & can be spread by aerosol [e.g. sneezing] or by contact with infected surfaces. This is why it spreads so quickly in closed environments such as hospital wards & classrooms. Controls include thorough cooking, avoiding risks of cross contamination, maintaining high standards of personal hygiene, especially handwashing & taking care when sourcing & preparing shellfish to be served raw.

Pathogenic micro-organisms

- *Staphylococcus aureus, Bacillus cereus*
  - produce toxins in food
  - generally cause vomiting
  - quick onset
- *Campylobacter jejuni, Salmonella, E. coli, Clostridium perfringens*
  - originate in the gut
  - generally cause diarrhoea
  - slower onset

Bacteria that produce toxins generally cause vomiting. The poison is in the food & the body responds quickly to get rid of it so the onset period is usually short, just a few hours

Bacteria that comes from the gut generally causes diarrhoea. The bacteria themselves produce a reaction in the intestines so the onset period is generally longer 12-36 hours sometimes in excess of 72 hours

All this makes it very difficult for an EHO [Environmental Health Officer] to investigate.

Could you remember exactly what you ate 72 hours ago?

Chapter 3a: Food Safety Hazards

Binary fission

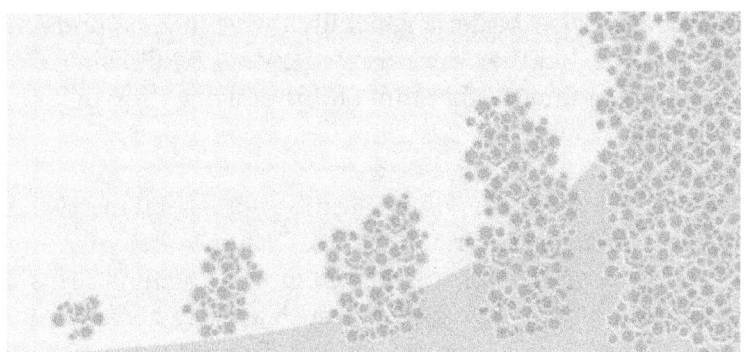

Binary fission means divide into two. One bacteria becomes two, two becomes four, four become eight, eight become sixteen & so on...

Under optimal conditions the microbes double within 20 minutes. After an additional 20 minutes there are 4 then 8, 16, 32, 64 ... after 10 hours there are 1,073,741,824 !!!

The Right Conditions

Food ~ Moisture ~ Warmth ~ Time

Given the right conditions, millions of bacteria can grow on common, everyday foods. These conditions are:

Food: nutrients – bacteria generally thrive in & on protein-based foods, but they can survive for days by utilising virtually anything; a thin film of dirt or a dry drop of blood for instance.

Moisture: is critical for multiplication – it is vital to dry surfaces to deny bacteria moisture. The sink area of a kitchen often harbours the highest level of bacteria. This includes moisture in 'wet' foods such as juicy meats, sandwich fillings, soups, sauces and dressings

Warmth: at what temperature do you think most bacteria will multiply quickest? Body temperature – 37°C [most food poisoning bacteria favour living in a host]

Time: Under optimum conditions bacteria can double every 10 to 20 minutes

For a healthy adult the probability of getting sick from contaminated food is dependent on both the type and number of harmful microorganisms present in the food. For those who are susceptible, namely the very young, and those who are sick or pregnant, where their immune systems are less effective, lower numbers of microorganisms may be required to cause illness

.

Danger Zone:

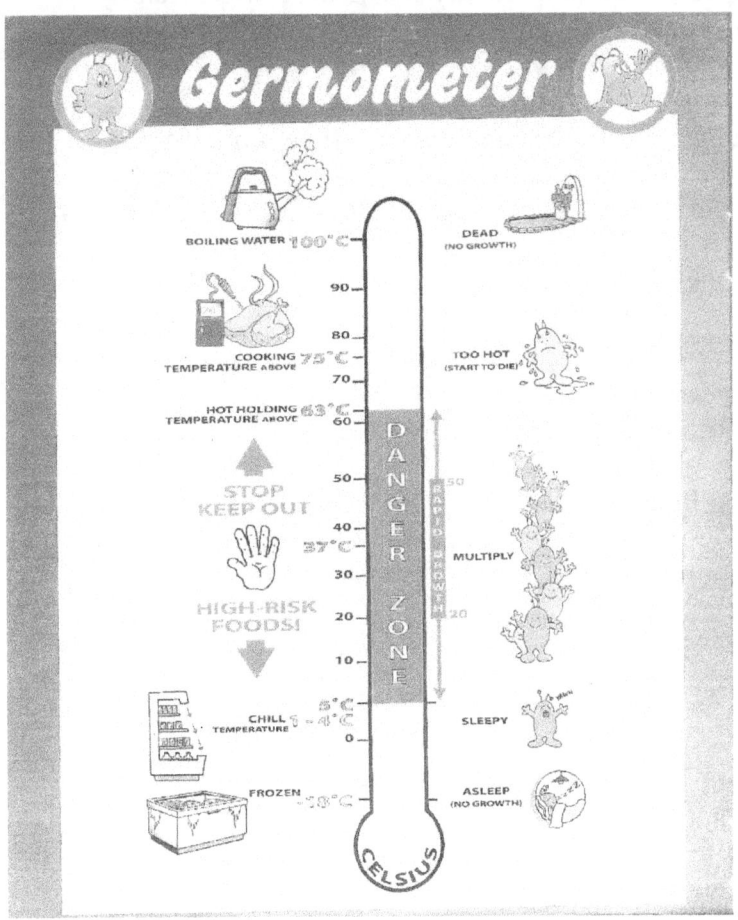

It is very important to remember these temperatures!

This germometer clearly shows the Danger Zone – the optimum temperature zone for cell multiplication ~ 5°C to 63°C

Freezer -18°C bacteria dormant do not multiply

Fridge / chiller 1°C – 5°C bacteria sleepy but not dead

Hot hold 63°C for two hours

Cook & kill bacteria 72°C to 75°C

Disinfect e.g. Dishwasher 82°C

Boiling will kill all bacteria except Clostridium botulinum
Minimum temperature to kill Clostridium botulinum spores: 100°C/212°F to 116°C/240°F

Spore-forming bacteria

The whole canning industry is based upon killing *Clostridium botulinum* spores. We are now ale to preserve meats & foodstuffs for a very long time

Spore forming bacteria cannot be killed on cooking; when they encounter unfavourable conditions they form spores [i.e. hide in protective casings] & wait until favourable conditions return so they can multiply again. Clostridium perfringens & Bacillus cereus are also spore forming bacteria

Stews, curries & sauces must be stirred well & continuously to prevent cold spots [danger zone]

Food must be cooled as rapidly as possible & placed in the refrigerator.

High-risk foods

What do these foods have in common?

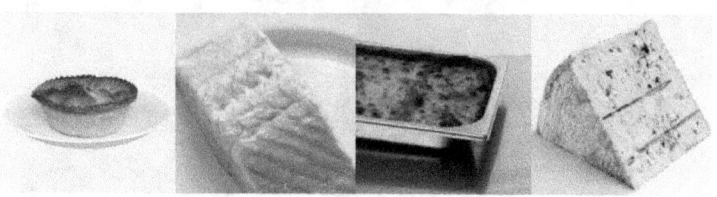

Meat pie, cooked salmon, prepared meal, cheese?

These are all ready to eat, moist, high in protein, require strict time & temperature control, short shelf life & require NO other process

You must remember this!

So, what about these foods? Are they High Risk?

Dried rice? Chicken sandwich? Bar of chocolate? Cooked hamburger? Raw chicken? Bag of crisps? Smoked salmon?

Dried rice, no because it is dry; chicken sandwich, yes it is ready to eat & moist; bar of chocolate, not high risk doesn't need to be kept in a fridge; cooked hamburger, yes ticks all the boxes, raw chicken, no it isn't ready to eat & cooking will kill the bacteria; bag of crisps, no because it is dry & salty; smoked salmon, yes ticks all the boxes

High risk food must be handled as little as possible & kept out of the danger zone

Cross-contamination

Raw to cooked food

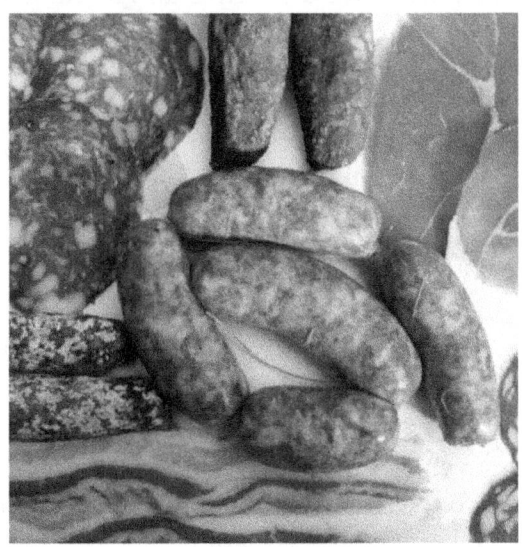

Direct contamination: blood drip, raw touching cooked

Indirect contamination: knife, cutting board, cloth

Cross contamination occurs when bacteria are transferred from a contaminated source e.g. from raw meat to a ready-to-eat product & usually involves a vehicle – hands, utensils & equipment, knives, cutting boards, handles of doors, fridges, cupboards

Cross contamination can be controlled by storing raw & ready to eat foods separately. In large premises there will be a separate chiller for each but in smaller outfits you must ensure that they are on different shelves in the chiller [raw below cooked]

Wash your hands after handling raw food & before handling read to eat food & vice versa.

Large factories will have different staff handling different processes & they may even wear different colour clothing e.g. red for meat preparation, white for diary, green for vegetable

Use tongs when handling high risk food & clean all utensils thoroughly between use.

Colour coded utensils & chopping boards can be used.

Cloths can be colour coded but disposable cloths or paper towels are preferable

All these are vehicles for contamination they involve hand contact & or food contact surfaces. There will be more about this in the chapter on cleaning

It is imperative to make sure bacteria in food do not rise to unsafe levels prior to eating. Refrigeration will impede both bacterial growth & toxin production

High risk foods cause most problems as they have all the right criteria for bacterial multiplication

Chapter 4: Taking Temperatures

A probe is used to record the temperature of food ~ here are two examples:

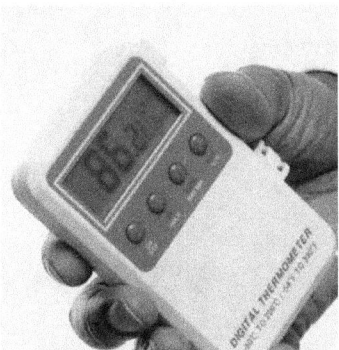

Hard Probe Thermometer

Infra-red [gun type] Probe Thermometer

Probes must be cleaned with hot water & detergent after use & disinfected with anti-bacterial probe wipes before using again

Using a Temperature Probe

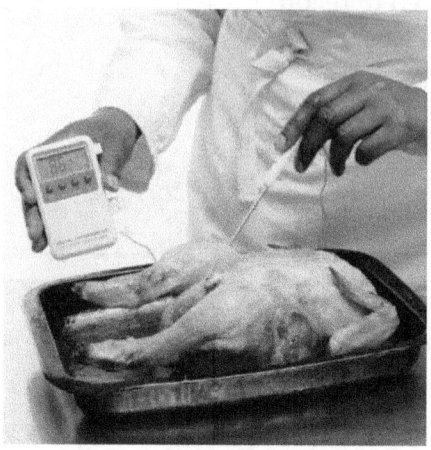

Every probe must be:
- properly calibrated
- cleaned and disinfected between use

If this is your job you must be fully trained in:

- how to check the temperature,
- record the temperature,
- what to do if the temperatures are unsafe or what to do if a reading is unsafe

Quarterly calibration is considered good practice in the industry.

Calibration is carried out by comparing the device with a reference thermometer that has been confirmed as accurate

Probes can be calibrated in the same way or by placing in ice & boiling water

Chapter 5: Refrigeration, chilling and cold holding of foods

Again, we are looking at the same stuff from a different angle

Chilled storage

At or below:
- 8°C – law
- 5°C – good practice

The Food Safety (Temperature Control) Regulations 1995 require that certain foods are kept at or below 8°C. It is recommended that refrigerators & chillers operate at between 2°C and 5°C. [https://www.rbkc.gov.uk/]

We always use 5°C in practice

Aim to cool food to 5°C or less within 90 minutes & put it in the refrigerator

Top and middle shelves
Ready-to-eat foods

Dairy products, yoghurts, cream, cream cakes, butter and margarine, cooked meats, leftovers (covered), other packaged food, for example coleslaw, ketchup, and so on.

Bottom shelf
Raw meat, poultry and fish

You should always cover raw meats, poultry and fish and keep them in sealed containers.

Salad drawer
Salad, vegetables and fruit

Keep ready-to-eat fruit and vegetables in sealed bags or containers. Always wash raw fruit and vegetables before use.

Do not put warm food in a refrigerator

A blast chiller is the best method of cooling food but if you don't have one:
- Divide a stew into smaller portions & put in shallow cold trays
- Place in an ice water bath
- Stir to speed up the process
- Make a concentrate product & add ice when reconstituting

Keep covered to protect from contamination

Cold hold e.g. on display for 4 hours max

Frozen storage

Wrap food to prevent:
- contamination
- freezer burn

At -18oC bacteria dormant, they cannot multiply

There are no defined temperatures for freezers but we recommend they operate at -18°C or below.
[https://www.rbkc.gov.uk/]

- Freeze as quickly as possible
- Store raw food below ready-to-eat/high risk foods
- Longest shelf-life behind/below shortest shelf-life
- Keep food in supplier's original packaging – once opened reseal with care
- If you re-wrap frozen food label it clearly & include a date mark

Thawing food

Check to ensure that food is properly thawed before cooking

Defrost in a chiller, microwave or specialist defrosting unit

Cover to prevent cross contamination

The container used for defrosting should be dedicated to the purpose & kept clean. Make sure the container is large enough to contain the thawing liquid. Check regularly to make sure it doesn't overflow & cause cross contamination.

Plan ahead so that you allow enough time for thorough thawing before cooking; a large turkey might need 24 hours or more

Do not re-freeze thawed food – each time food enters the danger zone the risk of food poisoning increases

Check before cooking that it is fully defrosted without ice particles. This can be done with a probe or by visual & manual checks. Make sure that poultry legs are pliable

If you cook food without it being completely defrosted it will not cook thoroughly. Bacteria may survive & multiply.

Checking & recording refrigerator temperatures

Fridge temperatures must be checked at least once a day; usually twice a day

It is the temperature of the food that is vital not the air temperature around it

It is good practice to use a [clearly labelled] product substitute if possible, which should remain in the chiller, in the warmest position, & be dedicated to probing alone. This reduces the risk of cross contamination but isn't practical in supermarkets.

Some units have temperature reading dials on the outside - never rely on them, always double check

Chapter 6: Cooking, Hot Holding & Reheating of Foods

First let's have a look at what you have learned so far.

What are the hazards you can spot in this picture?

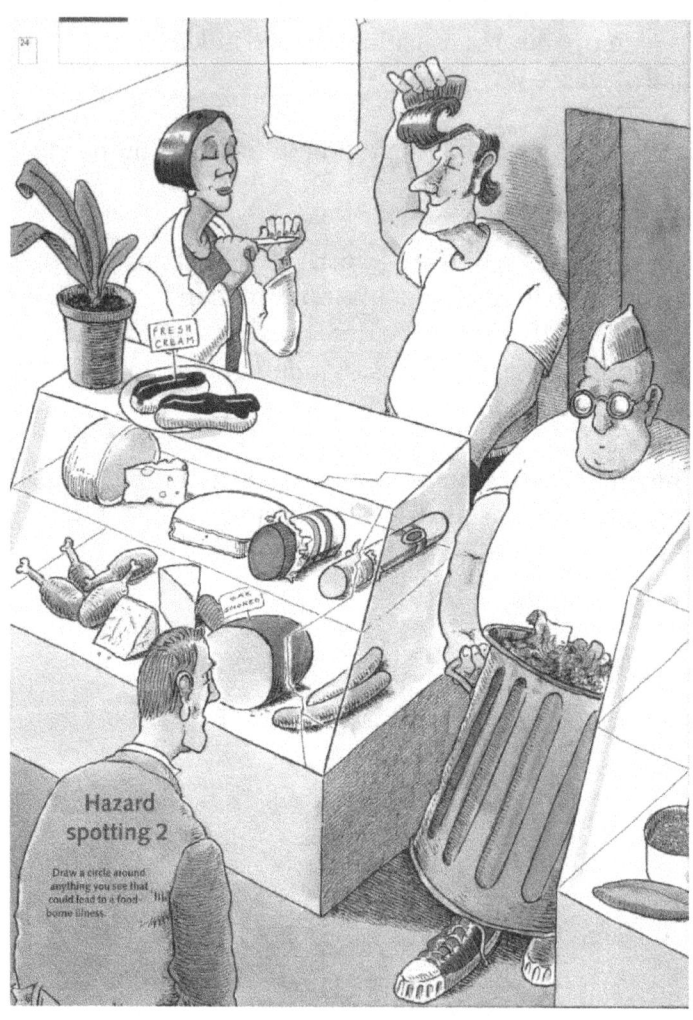

- Do not comb your hair anywhere near food

- You must not file your nails or wear earrings

- The plant must not be near food [clostridium perfringens/spore former in soil]

- Fresh cream chocolate eclairs in the danger zone sitting on the top of the cabinet

- Cracked cabinet will harbour bacteria

- Meats & cheeses must not be unwrapped near one another

- Cooked chicken must not be next to cheese

- Rubbish & waste must not be near food & the man taking out the bin is not wearing catering footwear & he may trip over his laces

- Notice on wall stuck with tape that might fall off & drop into the food

Cooking

Always check to ensure that you cook food thoroughly

Most bacteria are killed at 75°C

Stir or turn to ensure target temperature is consistent throughout the product

Leave microwaved food for 2 minutes after cooking to allow the temperature to equalise.

- Measure with clean probe
- Make sure meat juices run clear
- Make sure food is steaming hot
- Do not assume food is thoroughly cooked – you must check

- Cooking is a 'critical control point' in HACCP
- Due Diligence: recording temperatures help a business demonstrate that critical limits are being monitored.

It may not be necessary for every item of food to be probed depending on the rules in your place of work but temperatures must be recorded at the start of the day & at periodic times during the day

It would be a good idea to check that equipment is working efficiently by checking a sample from a batch. This is particularly important for grills, griddles & fryers

Reheating food

Reheat food to a minimum temperature of 75°C* ONCE only [* 82°C in Scotland]

Wherever possible do not cook, cool, store, & re-heat food. Cook & serve is the safest method.

What could happen if food is not reheated thoroughly?
- Bacteria survive
- Bacteria remain in the danger zone
- Bacteria multiply
- Spores germinate

If food is cooked, cooled & reheated it passes through the danger zone three times, giving more opportunity for bacteria to multiply & produce toxins.

Hot Holding

At or above 63°C

If the temperature of the food drops below 63°C it must be sold or served within 2 hours or destroyed.

A fast-moving service will ensure that most foods will not be hot held for very long but if any food remains at the end of service, it must be destroyed.

However, different businesses have different rules – it is important that you follow the procedures that apply in your workplace.

You can ensure that hot food is not held for too long by recording the time the food enters 'hot hold' & by holding small portions that are not topped up.

Re-Cap

Cooking is vital to kill bacteria

Core temp of 75oC for 30 seconds will ensure safety

Cooking & serving is the safest method of presenting food

Food may be cooked & re-heated ONCE only

Re-heat to at least 75oC

Hot hold 63oC – if food drops below this it must be served or disposed of within 2 hours

Go back & check the germometer

Cold hold 5oC ~ 4 hours

Hot hold 63oC ~ 2 hours

You have 90 minutes to cool food & put it in the fridge or freezer

Chapter 7: Food Handlers

Once again, we are looking at all the same stuff but from the angle of personal responsibility

Hand Washing

Is one of the most important actions you can take to help prevent contamination

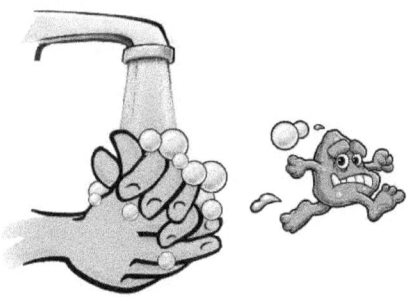

When should you wash your hands?

Before: Starting work
                Handling high risk food

After:

                Visiting the lavatory
                Handling raw eggs or raw food
                Coughing or sneezing
                Touching hair or face
                Cleaning or touching chemical containers
                Dealing with rubbish
                Eating, drinking, smoking

How to wash your hands

There is a whole science about how to wash your hands

Use liquid soap

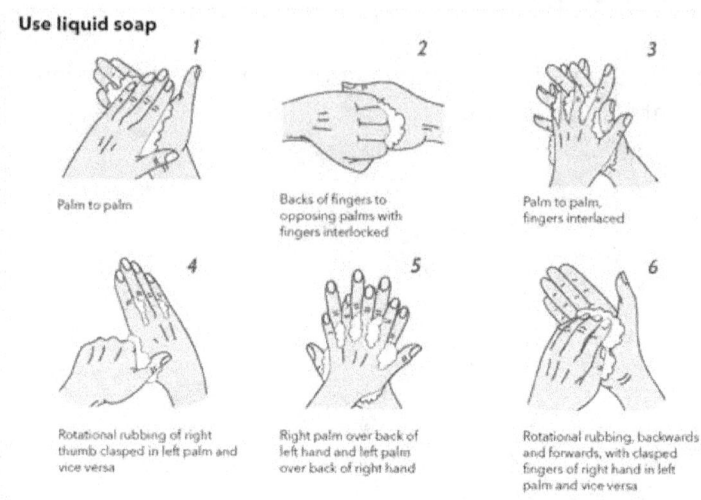

Rinse and dry your hands thoroughly

Always use a hand basin provided exclusively for washing hands

Use comfortably hot water rub your hands vigorously to work in the soap

Don't forget the areas in between your fingers and around your wrists

Rinse your hands before drying them

It is not only important to wash your hands but to wash them properly.

Work soap into your hands & do so vigorously for 20 seconds.

Clean the backs of your hands, between your fingers & your wrists.

Clean your nails with a nail brush, preferably as disposable one, especially after handling raw food.

It is equally important to rinse your hands before drying them using disposable paper towels.

Personal hygiene

You must maintain the highest possible standards of personal hygiene to avoid contaminating food

There is quite a lot to think about…

What protective clothing would food handlers wear?

What is the purpose of protective clothing?

What properties should protective clothing have?

Think about items of protective clothing & the reasons for wearing them

& what other procedures do you think food handlers ought to follow?

The purpose of protective clothing is to
 protect the food from the handler, not the other way around

The clothing properties should be light not dark so any dirt can be seen

It must be washable, without pockets or buttons, which could be physical contaminants & could be disposable

Hats & hairnets stop hands touching hair & ears [source of staphylococcus aureus] & stops hair falling into the food [physical contaminant]

Beard snood [same as above] for facial hair

An apron or chef jacket & trousers protect the food from any contaminant that might be on the food handlers' own clothes

Dedicated shoes or overshoes stops the transfer of contaminants from the soles of outdoor shoes from entering the kitchen. Also, for Health & Safety reasons they need to have non-slip soles

Gloves are to be worn:

- if the product being handled might cause dermatitis, or an allergic reaction
- when handling raw food
- when handling high risk food to act as a skin barrier
- when handling rubbish

If hands are kept clean there should be no need to wear gloves but you must follow your company policy

You might wear gloves if you have an allergic reaction to something like shellfish or when handling something highly coloured like beetroot which stains.

If you have a cut or lesion, a glove worn over a blue plaster ensures that the plaster cannot fall into the food but in this case, you must treat the glove in the same way as your hands & wash appropriately or discard & renew the glove.

Your responsibility:

It is important, & your responsibility as a food handler, to tell your manager, before starting work if you have suffered from diarrhoea, vomiting or skin problems

You must cover cuts & sores with waterproof, high visibility, dressings

You must not wear jewellery except a simple wedding band & 'sleeper' earrings. This rule will depend on your individual company policy

You must not wear nail polish, false nails or false eyelashes [physical contaminant]

Do not eat, drink or smoke while working. This prevents the transfer of bacteria from mouth to food.

Do not cough, spit, pick your nose or sneeze

Do not breathe on glassware or cutlery while you are polishing it up

If you are going to test or taste food, always use a clean spoon. Never use your fingers.

Remember ~ it is your responsibility to record any illness

Chapter 8: Principles of Safe Storage

This may appear to be repeating stuff we have already covered but it is important to learn all aspects of food safety from every angle

Preservation

Preservation methods remove one or more requirement for bacterial growth

Remember ??? What are the ideal conditions that bacteria need to grow & multiply?

Food ~ Moisture ~ Warmth ~ Time

All foods decompose due to the action of spoilage bacteria. We can extend the life of food by preserving. Here are a number of different methods:

- Drying – removes moisture
- Freezing – removes moisture & warmth
- Chilling – removes warmth
- Pickling – removes moisture chemically
- Vacuum packing – removes oxygen or substitutes gases required for metabolism – aerobic/anaerobic bacteria
- Sterilisation/UHT/canning/irradiation – kills any form of life
- Smoking - & associated drying removes moisture – chemicals in the smoke also directly kill some micro organisms

It is sometimes thought that vacuum packed products can be kept at ambient temperatures but this is mostly incorrect. High risk food such a smoked salmon for instance must be refrigerated even if it is vacuum packed.

Always check storage instructions on any food label

Date marking

Government advice says firms should include only use-by or best-before dates and remove sell-by and display-until labels relating to stock control. The UK throws away about £12bn of edible food each year and critics say confusing packaging is partly to blame.

Use-by date on ready-to-eat foods – It is a criminal offence to sell food past its use-by date

Use-by dates are used on high risk foods likely to cause food poisoning. To re-cap, high risk foods are ready to eat, high in protein, moist, require chilling & have a short shelf life.

By exceeding the use-by date such foods have exceeded the critical time limit within which the product might be considered safe. Thereafter the bacterial load might be sufficient to cause food poisoning.

What should you do if you find food that is past it's use-by date?

At this food safety basic level, as an employee you must report it to your manager. It has to be disposed of immediately. If any enforcement officer finds food, past it's use-by date, in a business premises, he or she will presume it to be for sale; unless clearly marked otherwise "not for human consumption". The business owner could be subject to a criminal prosecution.

Best-before date – mainly found on canned, dried and frozen products – It is not an offence for products to be sold beyond the best-before date, but safety and quality could be compromised

Biscuits may go rancid & soggy, tea will become dry & powdery, tins might become damaged & 'blow' [damage allows air in & pressurizes the contents]

Stock rotation

FIFO – 'first in first out' – is the golden rule of stock rotation

Stock rotation is undertaken to ensure that food is safe & not wasted.   Use products with shorter shelf life first by bringing them to the front of the shelf & place those with longer lives at the back.

This rule applies to dry storage, refrigerated storage & frozen

Chilled Storage

- Clean and defrost thoroughly
- Cover and label food
- Keep food tidy
- Don't over stock
- FIFO
- No warm food
- Separate raw and ready-to-eat foods
- Decant food from metal containers
- Keep food away from fans

Check temperatures for goods in if chilled or frozen & make sure they are within the limits set in your business. If they are not you will probably have to reject them, depending on your individual business procedures. Always check with your supervisor.

When handling goods that would normally be refrigerated always ensure they are put back into the refrigerator as quickly as possible

Frozen storage

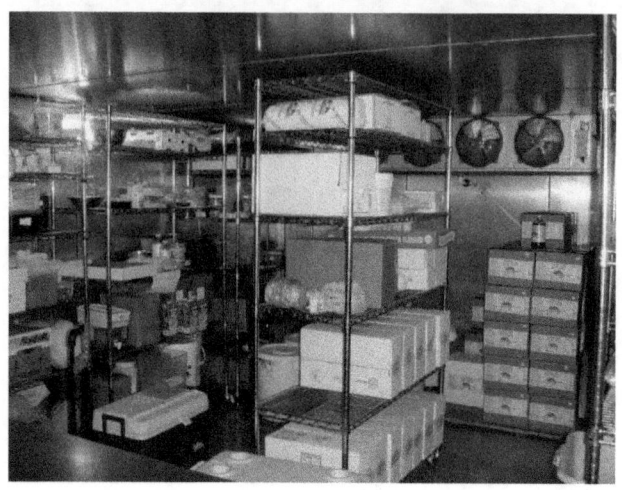

- Clean and defrost thoroughly
- Cover and label food
- Keep food tidy
- Don't over stock
- No warm food
- FIFO

Ensure adequate temperature records are kept; during the day & when goods arrive

Dry Goods Storage

This refers to any foodstuffs that do not require refrigeration or freezing...

FIFO [first in first out] also applies

- Ventilated, clean and light
- Off the floor and away from walls
- Stock control and checks
- Designated area for returns or discarded stock

Ventilation is important as it helps air circulating & keeps moulds & fungi from building up

Light is important to be able to check for cleanliness & signs of pest infestation & to be able to read date marks easily

Stock must be kept off the floor & away from walls to allow cleaning underneath & to prevent pests from making nests in undisturbed areas

Chapter 9: Food Allergy & Intolerance

Regulations

There are new regulations on the way allergens are labelled on pre-packed foods.

The Food Information Regulation, which came into force in December 2014, introduced a requirement that food businesses must provide information about the allergenic ingredients used in any food they sell or provide.

There are 14 major allergens which need to be mentioned (either on a label or through provided information such as menus) when they are used as ingredients in a food.

Here are the allergens & some examples of where they can be found:

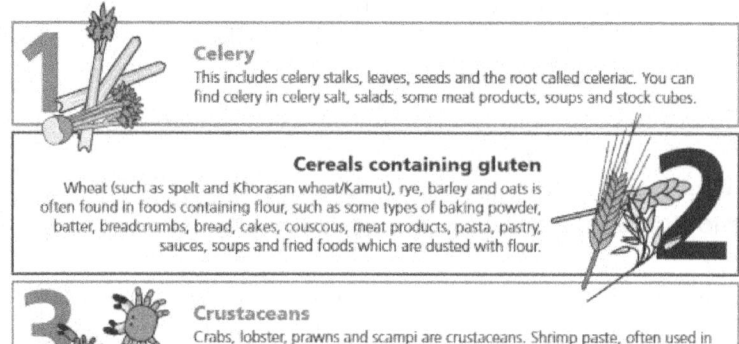

Celery
This includes celery stalks, leaves, seeds and the root called celeriac. You can find celery in celery salt, salads, some meat products, soups and stock cubes.

Cereals containing gluten
Wheat (such as spelt and Khorasan wheat/Kamut), rye, barley and oats is often found in foods containing flour, such as some types of baking powder, batter, breadcrumbs, bread, cakes, couscous, meat products, pasta, pastry, sauces, soups and fried foods which are dusted with flour.

Crustaceans
Crabs, lobster, prawns and scampi are crustaceans. Shrimp paste, often used in Thai and south-east Asian curries or salads, is an ingredient to look out for.

Eggs

Eggs are often found in cakes, some meat products, mayonnaise, mousses, pasta, quiche, sauces and pastries or foods brushed or glazed with egg.

 **4**

5 Fish

You will find this in some fish sauces, pizzas, relishes, salad dressings, stock cubes and Worcestershire sauce.

Lupin

Yes, lupin is a flower, but it's also found in flour! Lupin flour and seeds can be used in some types of bread, pastries and even in pasta.

  **6**

7 Milk

Milk is a common ingredient in butter, cheese, cream, milk powders and yoghurt. It can also be found in foods brushed or glazed with milk, and in powdered soups and sauces.

Molluscs

These include mussels, land snails, squid and whelks, but can also be commonly found in oyster sauce or as an ingredient in fish stews

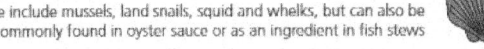  **8**

9 Mustard

Liquid mustard, mustard powder and mustard seeds fall into this category. This ingredient can also be found in breads, curries, marinades, meat products, salad dressings, sauces and soups.

Nuts

Not to be mistaken with peanuts (which are actually a legume and grow underground), this ingredient refers to nuts which grow on trees, like cashew nuts, almonds and hazelnuts. You can find nuts in breads, biscuits, crackers, desserts, nut powders (often used in Asian curries), stir-fried dishes, ice cream, marzipan (almond paste), nut oils and sauces.

 **10**

11 Peanuts

Peanuts are actually a legume and grow underground, which is why it's sometimes called a groundnut. Peanuts are often used as an ingredient in biscuits, cakes, curries, desserts, sauces (such as satay sauce), as well as in groundnut oil and peanut flour.

Sesame seeds

These seeds can often be found in bread (sprinkled on hamburger buns for example), breadsticks, houmous, sesame oil and tahini. They are sometimes toasted and used in salads.

 **12**

13 Soya
Often found in bean curd, edamame beans, miso paste, textured soya protein, soya flour or tofu, soya is a staple ingredient in oriental food. It can also be found in desserts, ice cream, meat products, sauces and vegetarian products.

Sulphur dioxide (sometimes known as sulphites)
This is an ingredient often used in dried fruit such as raisins, dried apricots and prunes. You might also find it in meat products, soft drinks, vegetables as well as in wine and beer. If you have asthma, you have a higher risk of developing a reaction to sulphur dioxide.

14

Allergic reactions include:

- Tingling round the mouth
- Swelling round the mouth, nose & throat
- Difficulty in breathing
- Rashes
- Vomiting
- Diarrhoea
- Abdominal cramps

Severe anaphylactic reactions can occur which cause the blood pressure & heart rate to be dangerously low. Without treatment, affected individuals can die within minutes.

People with allergies need to know that they food they eat is free from even the tiniest level of the relevant allergen

As a food handler you must be very careful not to inadvertently contaminate food that is supposed to be free of allergens. Use the same rules to prevent contamination as discussed previously.

Thorough hand & equipment washing is needed & the use of separate areas for preparation & production are required.

You must also be very careful to give the right information to customers who ask. Never guess; always ask your supervisor if you are unsure.

It is an offence to sell unsafe food; this includes giving the wrong information regarding the presence of an allergen in food by a misleading or incorrect label on the food, on a menu or verbally.

Chapter 10:   Cleaning

Again, everything we have learned earlier but from the point of view of cleaning

Dirty Premises

Would you like to work in premises likes this? Would you like to have a meal in a restaurant where the kitchen floor is in this state?

"Disgusting pictures have exposed a mouse-infested restaurant. They were slammed for "scamming the public" with a presentable façade when in fact its kitchens were infested with rodents.

The business was fined £14,000 and ordered to pay £7,000 in costs at Liverpool Magistrates' Court after pleading guilty to 10 charges of breaching health and safety legislation. The company had ignored warnings from its own pest control contractors that the restaurant's lack of cleanliness meant the infestation could not be controlled."

Source: https://www.mirror.co.uk/news/uk-news/disgusting-pictures-show-mouse-infestation-8873011

We prevent this from happening in our own workplace by cleaning thoroughly. We will now go through every aspect of cleaning

Detergent

What is a detergent?

A detergent is used to dissolve grease and remove dirt = visibly clean

Disinfectant

A disinfectant is used to reduce micro-organisms [bacteria] to safe levels. Not destroy – reduce to a safe level.

There are also products that combine the two called a sanitiser. A sanitiser cleans & disinfects.

Sterilization

Another method is sterilization which removes all micro organisms including spores. It is rarely used in catering but in the past, especially in hospitals, kitchens were fitted with sterilizing sinks fed with steam & hot water.

To clean or disinfect?

It is important to remember that even if something looks clean it could still be contaminated.

Let us now consider different types of objects & surfaces & decide which needs cleaning, & which needs cleaning & disinfecting.

Cleaning:

Floor
Walls
Ceilings
Under sides of work surfaces

Cleaning & disinfecting:

Taps
Knives
Chopping boards
Work surface
Fridge handle
Light switch
Splash back behind sink [maybe contaminated by splashes]
Bin lid
Mixing bowls

These are all hand &/or food contact surfaces which are often vehicles for contamination.

When using detergents, disinfectants & sanitisers you must never mix them

You must always follow the instructions on the label

Measure & use the correct concentration

Apply for the correct amount of time & rinse

Store away from foods in a designated area

The Six Stages of Wet Cleaning

Clean as you Go is a technical term.

We generally all do it at home as our mothers taught us but it is a food safety term & good practice.

1 Prepare ~ that is scrape everything off plates & out of saucepans; remove loose & heavy soiling
2 Clean ~ using hot water & detergent
3 Rinse ~ using clean hot water to remove any traces of detergent
4 Disinfect ~ use a chemical disinfectant & leave for the correct contact time or use extremely hot water
5 Final rinse ~ use clean hot water
6 Dry ~ if possible, leave to dry naturally in the air. If you use a cloth use a disposable paper towel or a clean fabric cloth only used once before being laundered again

Cloths

Cloths are a common source of contamination, so single-use, disposable cloths are recommended

If these are not available you need to make sure that the cloths you use are clean & fit for purpose.

Different types of cloths are used for different types of jobs.

Tea towels,
Chefs' cloths for holding hot items
Dish cloths for washing up dishes
Single use cloths for wiping surfaces, wiping up spills, wiping hands & wiping sides of dishes before serving

Due diligence & your defence in law:

Cleaning schedules detail cleaning tasks to be done at regular intervals, not covered by clean as you go activities during the normal course of the working day

The intervals could be daily for floors & bins, weekly for the insides of the refrigerators monthly or quarterly for ceilings behind racking etc.

The cleaning schedule includes the following information:

- The item or area to be cleaned
- The interval at which the item or area should be cleaned
- The method – the chemicals to be used, the protective clothing required, the safety precautions to be taken
- The name of the staff member responsible
- The name of the staff member to carry out the task
- The name of the person responsible for checking that the task has been carried out in accordance with the instructions

Or

The name of the contractors who carry out specialist cleaning tasks

A cleaning schedule is about what needs to be done & how; it is different from a cleaning record

A cleaning record is to enable staff & management to keep track of who has done the cleaning task, when it was done & if it was completed to the correct standards

The business owner is responsible for drawing up the cleaning schedule

Food handlers & kitchen porters are usually responsible for completing the task assigned to them

Washing Facilities

Hand wash facilities with hot & cold water, soap & drying facilities should be situated in a place that is conveniently accessible by food handlers

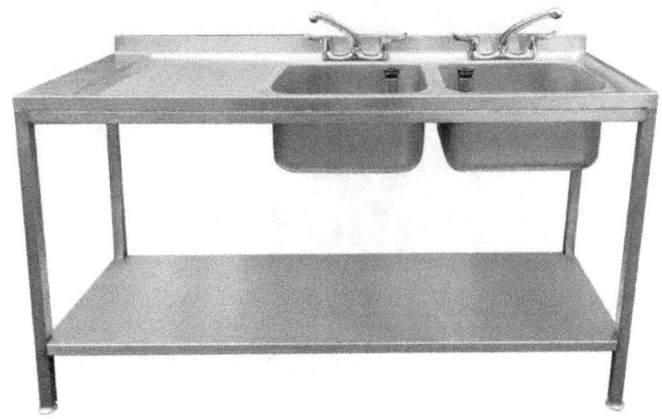

Separate food and equipment sinks with hot and cold water are required although in very small businesses the same sink could be used if the activities are separated by time & cleaning

Food businesses are required by law to provide these two however the ideal would be three. It would be good to have a separate sink for cleaning so you would not have to clean & disinfect everything time & time again after you have cleaned the floors for instance

Waste Disposal

Bins and waste are reservoirs of contamination & need to be treated accordingly

Waste must be kept in containers that are pest proof
Change refuse bags within bins in the kitchen regularly & keep lids on to ensure flies & other pests are not attracted
Clean refuse bins regularly & always wash hands after handling rubbish
Waste must not be allowed to accumulate it must be collected from your premises regularly
Waste of animal origin may need specialist waste contractors to collect them. For instance, some large restaurants are required to have separate collections for meat waste

If you have to handle rubbish bags while wearing chef whites you need to wear a disposable plastic apron & disposable gloves. These would be thrown away once the rubbish had been disposed of

Remember we keep the food safe & away from you the handler

To re-cap

Food premises need to be clean & abide by the law to avoid contaminating food

Some items & areas require cleaning & some require cleaning & disinfecting

Hand & food contact surfaces require cleaning & disinfection [these can act as vehicles of contamination]

Cleaning schedules help businesses run more effectively by identifying what needs cleaning, how often, by what method, & by whom

There are certain legal requirements that must be abided by in relation to cleaning, cleanliness, the provision of washing facilities, hands, food, & equipment in food businesses

Chapter 11:   Food Premises & Equipment

Design of Premises

We need to think of how we would design & equip our ideal premises.   Which would be the best materials to use?

Designed, constructed and equipped to minimise the risk of contamination

Worktops surfaces floor coverings would you have opening windows? Lots of things to consider

Premises must be suitable for the type of food being prepared

The design & construction must minimize the risk of contamination

The design must enable staff to clean easily & thoroughly

The best materials for the construction of food premises are durable, impervious, smooth & easy to clean

Food equipment & utensils must also be durable, impervious, smooth & easy to clean & resistant to cracking or chipping

Stainless steel is perfect for worktops

Nonstick/slip flooring

White paint – everything can be seen including rat runs smear marks should they ever get in

No windows – if there are opening windows, they must be covered by a pest proof grille or screen

First Aid Kit

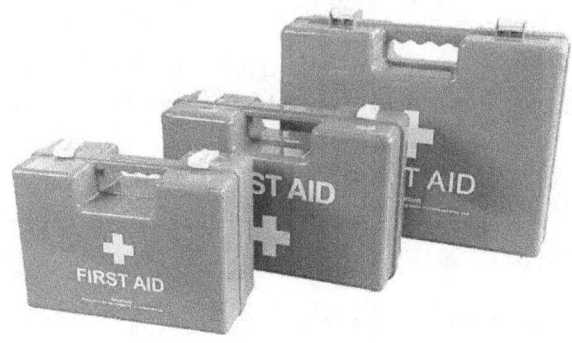

The law requires businesses to have adequate and appropriate first aid equipment, facilities and fully trained personnel on site to enable first aid to be given

In smaller businesses this means that someone could be appointed to take charge of the first aid kit & call an ambulance if needed

In larges businesses & factories one or more qualified first aiders will be required – the number depending on the size of the business & the associated risks

The most common injuries in kitchens are minor & deep cuts, burns & scalds, slips & trips & falls, sprains & strains

A First Aid Kit must have:

- Guidance card on basic first aid
- Individually wrapped sterile adhesive dressings – brightly coloured [blue] with/without thin metal strip
- Sterile eye pads
- Individually wrapped triangular bandages
- Safety pins
- Individually wrapped sterile unmedicated wound dressings
- Disposable gloves
- Bandages
- Scissors

The reason for having brightly coloured adhesive dressings is so that they can be easily seen & identified if they dropped into a stew, chutney or a meal

The reason for having a thin metal strip concealed within the dressing is because in some very large factories – the last thing that happens in a production line e.g. jars of chutney on conveyor belt – is that they go under a metal detector. If the alarms were set off, they would know that somewhere in a particular pot there was a blue plaster

If either of these scenarios occurred the whole batch of food would have to be destroyed – physical contaminant

Chapter 11:   Food Pests & Pest Control

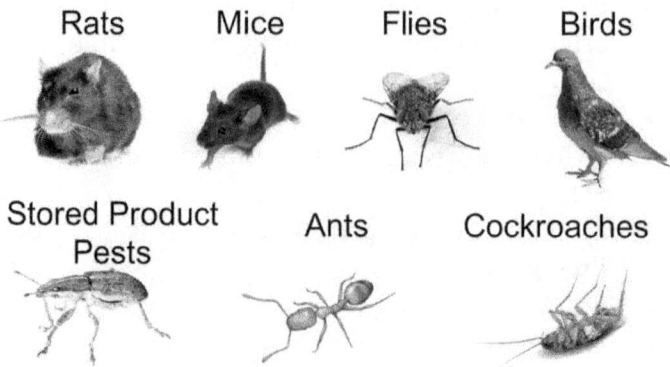

Rats   Mice   Flies   Birds

Stored Product   Ants   Cockroaches
Pests

These are the most common but there are many different types of pests that can destroy a food business. & cause illness

Pests thrive if they can find food, moisture, warmth and shelter – very similar to bacteria [food moisture warmth & time]

What is the official definition of a food pest? "A food pest is any creature that lives on or in human food causing damage or contamination or both"

The most common being rats, mice, cockroaches, birds, ants, flies & stored product pests, silverfish &mites. The list might also include animals that scavenge food businesses for example squirrels, foxes, seagulls

Pests survive if they can find:

Food ~ like rubbish or dirty surface

Moisture ~ like a dripping tap

Warmth ~ anywhere like hiding behind sacks of rice on the floor or behind a radiator

Shelter ~ as in quiet undisturbed corners [rarely moved racking rarely cleaned]

Store products off the floor & keep premises spotlessly clean

Food Pests

- transmit disease
- contaminate food (bodies, hair, faeces, urine)
- damage the structure of premises and equipment

Signs of infestation... Must be reported to the manager/supervisor

- Live or dead bodies
- Droppings
- Unusual smells
- Scratching, pecking or gnawing sounds
- Gnawed pipes, cables, fittings, bricks etc
- Torn or damaged packaging
- Spilled food
- Eggs, larvae, pupae, feathers, fur, nesting material
- Paw or claw prints
- Smears & rat runs

Stocks must be checked regularly especially dried products.

Noticing something moving in a bag of rice would be a sign of a stored product pest like a flour beetle which is only the size of a grain of rice

IDENTIFICATION OF COMMON PESTS OF STORED GRAIN
The following flow chart provides a useful guide for grain pest identification.

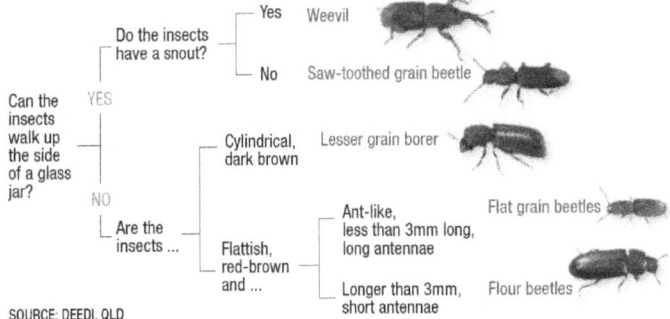

SOURCE: DEEDI, QLD

- damage to stored products, such as small holes in nuts or grain;
- live or dead insects (small beetles and moths), larvae, pupae or silken webbing on food storage bins;
- infestation, holes, larvae or webbing on the outside of packets or bags;
- larvae, pupae or silken webbing in food harbourages in cracks and crevices around shelves or on machinery;
- larvae, pupae or silken webbing in food spillages;
- larvae, pupae or silken webbing on beams and window sills;
- pests caught in insect traps.

Gnawed pipes, cables & fittings would be signs of rats –
rats have to gnaw continuously to keep their incisor teeth
worn down. Rat urine transmits Weils disease

Mice can get in anywhere they can get through the size of
a pencil, they have collapsible skulls & urinate
continuously

Cockroaches

- Diseases and allergens: cockroaches can carry a large number of disease-causing bacteria, including *Salmonella, Staphylococcus, Listeria, E. coli*, and also fungi, viruses and parasitic worms;
- They feed on decaying matter, mould, faecal matter in sewers, from rodents and birds, and animal carcasses, which can then be transmitted into the food production environment on their bodies or from excreta;
- They defecate along their pathways;
- They frequently expel saliva on surfaces to 'taste' their environment;
- Droppings and bodily secretions stain and leave a foul odour that can permeate infestation areas, food and packaging;
- Discarded, cast skins and egg cases contaminate products and packaging;
- Droppings and shed skins contain allergens, and heavy cockroach populations can trigger asthma attacks.

Rats

Rodents transmit a large number of diseases, including Salmonellosis, Leptospirosis, Toxoplasmosis, Lyme disease, rat-bite fever;

Rodents carry ectoparasites, including ticks, fleas, lice and mites and are therefore also vectors for the diseases that these carry.

Rodents are reservoirs for some mosquito-borne diseases.

If left unchecked, a pair of rats can produce 482,508,800 descendants in just three years
Rat pregnancy lasts 21-23 days, with a female rat typically birthing six litters per year, consisting of 5-10 pups

When a female mouse becomes pregnant, it only takes between 19 and 21 days for her to give birth to a litter. Each litter typically consists of five or six mouse pups, though it's not rare to see as many as 12 in a litter.

A typical female mouse can birth between five and 10 litters per year. She can mate immediately after giving birth, meaning mice can give birth to a second litter in as little as 25 days after the first. This cycle continues until the mouse dies. By then, her grandaughters have also birthed a few litters, which are starting to breed.

Flies

They feed on faecal matter, garbage, rotting materials as well as stored and processed foods in food processing plants.

They will regularly move between the contaminated food sources and clean areas, carrying contaminated filth on their bodies as well as microorganisms internally.

Many types of fly have hair like structures on their bodies, hairs and sticky pads on their feet and deeply channelled mouth parts that can pick up contaminated material as they feed.

Also flies such as house flies regurgitate digestive juices and defecate while feeding and resting, contaminating foods and surfaces with microorganisms that can cause disease or decay.

Fruit flies are not generally considered to be as great a health risk as other flies because they are not thought of as filth feeders. However, they do need a protein supply to produce eggs and this can be animal faeces.

Birds

The most common bird pests are pigeons, house sparrows, seagulls and starlings.

Birds can cause physical damage by dislodging roof tiles, particularly the larger birds, and blocking guttering with nests and feathers.

They produce substantial amounts of droppings which foul buildings, vehicles, paved areas and building entrances.

Inside buildings, bird droppings, nesting material and feathers can contaminate surfaces, machinery and food products.

Apart from being unsightly, birds can transmit many human pathogens including viruses, bacteria, fungi and protozoa. More common microorganisms include *Salmonella*, *E coli* and *Campylobacter*.

Bird nesting and roosting sites also encourage infestations, of arthropods such as bird mites, fleas and some beetle species.

Moths

- Indian meal moth: nuts, dried fruit and grain.
- Mill moth: flour.
- Tropical warehouse moth: stored cereal, nuts, dried fruit, oil seeds and oil cakes.
- Warehouse moth: cocoa beans, chocolate confectionery, dried fruit and nuts.

Beetles & weevils

- There is a very large number of species of beetle and weevil that feed on dried foods such as: cereals/grains, flour, seeds, nuts, pulses, dried fruit, chocolate, spices and processed products including pasta.

Mites

- Cheese mite: cheese, nuts, dried eggs, fruit, flour, tobacco.
- Flour or grain mites: cereals, dried vegetable materials, cheese, corn and dried fruits

Pest Damage Illustration:

"Waltham Forest Council food safety officers discovered mice, rat and cockroach infestations at Ruby's Grill in High Road, Leyton, during an inspection earlier this month.

Officers were dismayed to find that an intrusion of cockroaches had made a home out of a box containing chef hygiene hats.

Mice and rat droppings were discovered in close proximity to food preparation areas and officers documented rancid grease dripping from pipes.

A special health and safety prohibition order was served preventing people from walking across an upstairs floor as rats had gnawed beams so extensively that it may have caused a ceiling collapse. Officers also made checks on surrounding businesses to ensure they were not at risk. "source: http://www.yellowad.co.uk/

It is very important to prevent a visit from a food pest!

Pest Control

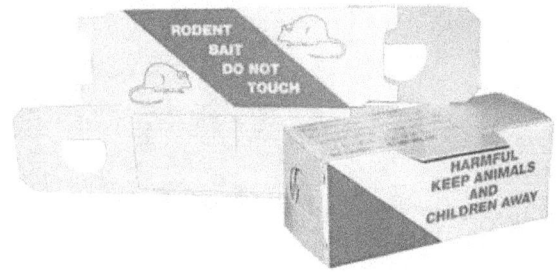

Don't interfere with pest prevention measures or equipment. Never touch or move them.

It may be that the company you work for employs a pest control contractor & that will be their 'due diligence' in law or you might have someone in your company designated to take on this role

Pest control equipment includes:

Electronic fly killers
Monitors – bait & sticky surfaces
Traps – sticky traps cockroaches get stuck
Insecticide sprays – definitely never to be used anywhere near food [chemical contaminant] only used in a food business when it has been completely closed down
Pesticide baits
Shoots [bird pests]

At this level, if you see signs of food pests, your responsibility is to tell your supervisor

So, what have we learned?

Which hazards can you identify here?

Answers:

Temperature on outside of fridge at 11°C too high must be -5°C or it might be a freezer where the temperature must be -18°C

Guy picking his spots

Potatoes on the floor

Cat in the kitchen

Food in boxes defrosting on the floor

Rat behind the door

Rubbish/waste sacks in kitchen

Fridge/freezer defrosting

Bread delivery on the floor

Open window near waste bin – flies entering kitchen

Act to ensure that the food you make, serve or sell is safe to eat

& then you will have a thriving business, or work for one, & not one that is likely to be closed down

Well Done!

You have completed all the information needed

Now...all you have to do is sit the Examination & gain your Certificate

About

Hello, my name is Susie Ellis, mother of four, a qualified hypnotherapist & business & lifestyle coach.

I started my working life as a PA for a commercial Estate Agent in Green Park, London & then when I later moved to Norfolk, I became PA to the Finance Director of a Blue-Chip Company. The first gave me hands on experience in a start-up & the second a fantastic grounding in the 'bottom line'.

During a management buy-out, another fantastic learning curve, I found myself being eased sideways so I left & started up my own business as a consultant.

My first project was to overhaul all the working processes & systems for a company specialising in laying oil pipelines in Russia! It was a fixed 6 month contract & I then had to employ staff to take over the running of the company. Since then I have specialised in troubleshooting.

I worked with CRISIS the charity for the homeless as food services co-ordinator for many years, obtained the Advanced Certificate in Food Safety & taught food safety to volunteers for the COC [Crisis Open Christmas] & to private clients

In 2010 I qualified as a hypnotherapist & I now use those skills, including NLP, in my coaching business. I find that mindset & self-esteem are as important to a business as financial reporting.

We specialise in helping people and businesses excel in all that they do.   We can help you achieve…providing accountability, guidance, systems & ideas

Also, over the years I have become more & more interested in maintaining a healthy lifestyle, eating organic & unprocessed food & avoiding pharmaceuticals.

I have developed a lifelong interest in food & it's effect on our health which began when one of my children was cured of 'hyperactivity syndrome' by cutting out food additives & colourings from his diet…see www.susieellis.org

Then I progressed to researching the ingredients in the personal care products & makeup we were using. I was horrified to read about SLS & Propylene glycol for a start! Let alone what else I uncovered during the process…

I was encouraged to learn the truth, help others, & share my findings & ideas with the world…see www.behindthetruth.co.uk

Contact me:

I am more than happy to answer questions & hear your experiences
so do get in touch...

email: info@susieellis.net

or find me on Facebook
www.facebook.com/susieellis.inc

or Twitter @_SusieEllis

Disclaimer

The entire contents of this book & related programme are based solely upon the opinions & views of the author unless otherwise noted. Individual articles are based upon the opinions of the respective author, who retains copyright as marked. The information in this book, programme & website is not intended to replace a one to one relationship with a qualified health care professional and is not intended as medical advice. It is intended as a sharing of knowledge and information from the research and experience of Susie Ellis and the wider community.

Copyright

Credits & references

Photo credits:

Freezer burn Steven Depolo, Flickr
Thawing food WikiHow
Fridge www.safefood.eu
Tin cans www.pixnio.com
Cooking pots Timus Saglambilek, Pexels
Hot holding Westchester food safety NYC
Hand washing www.cdifffoundation.org
Handwashing routine Isle of Man www.gov.im
Chef jacket www.yarmo.co.uk
Use by date Daily Mail
Best before www.collectivepurchasing.co.uk
Supermarket shelves www.freepik.com
Walk in fridge & walk in freezer www.blog.shelving.com
Dry goods shelving https://action-storage.com
Allergen images www.food.gov.uk/allergy
Kitchen floor Liverpool Echo
Detergent & disinfectant www.cleaningproductsuk.com
High Risk Foods, Six stages of cleaning CIEH level 2
award in food safety
Cloths www.jumia.co.ke
Hand wash sink www.cs-catering-equipment.co.uk
Commercial sinks www.professionalkitchens.co.uk/
Bin bag Wellpack Europe @ amazon.co.uk
Stainless steel kitchen www.indiamart.com
First aid kit http://www.safetyfirstaid.co.uk
Stored grain pests http://storedgrain.com.au
Rat damage www.totalpestcontrolsolutions.co.uk/
Rodent bait Rentokil.co.uk
Binary fission http://www.grotamar.com
Mouse in loaf
https://www.theguardian.com/lifeandstyle/gallery/2012
/sep/19/food-with-unexpected-animal-extras

Hazard spotting, quiz, sausages, probes, natural poisons ~
CIEH level 2 award in food safety

References:

Pest control information source:
https://www.rentokil.co.uk/food-processing/pests-in-food-processing/

www.ingramcontent.com/pod-product-compliance
Lightning Source LLC
Chambersburg PA
CBHW072148170526
45158CB00004BA/1559